ABANDONED
VERMONT

ABANDONED
VERMONT

DISHEVELMENT IN THE GREEN MOUNTAINS

MAXWELL BRISBEN

AMERICA
THROUGH TIME®
ADDING COLOR TO AMERICAN HISTORY

America Through Time is an imprint of Fonthill Media LLC
www.through-time.com
office@through-time.com

Published by Arcadia Publishing by arrangement with Fonthill Media LLC
For all general information, please contact Arcadia Publishing:
Telephone: 843-853-2070
Fax: 843-853-0044
E-mail: sales@arcadiapublishing.com
For customer service and orders:
Toll-Free 1-888-313-2665

www.arcadiapublishing.com

First published 2020

Copyright © Maxwell Brisben 2020

ISBN 978-1-63499-225-1

Typeset in Trade Gothic 10pt on 15pt
Printed and bound in England

ACKNOWLEDGMENTS

THANK YOU to my parents, for without their support over all these years none of this would be possible.

A special thank you to Juliana Skelly, for literally keeping my footing and being right there with me in exploring these places.

As a January snow squall looms over Mount Mansfield, a farmer rolls past with some bales of hay. At 4,395 feet, it is Vermont's highest peak. From this angle, you would never know it is home to a world-class ski resort.

CONTENTS

INTRODUCTION

When I first learned how to compose a photograph, I did it because I wanted to share the natural beauty of the stunning state I grew up in. I was born in New Jersey, but that is not who I am. I feel very lucky to have lived here as long as I have, and to have the comfort of the woods always close at hand.

After one too many sunset landscapes, I changed my focus to the myriad of abandoned places around the state. I wanted to get up close and personal. I wanted to go inside and get a read for these spaces—to take their temperature and document them accordingly. The poetry followed to provide the sounds, smells, and feelings that photography can lack.

Many times, I will return to document these locations throughout the seasons and years to see how they change. It also gives me an opportunity to thoroughly observe and document the entirety of the objects and detail within, attaining a visual texture of the space.

Sometimes, I feel like they call me back, and I am welcomed when I step back inside. The thresholds I cross are the reason that I regularly document windows and doorways because the idea of a defined boundary between outside and in is so straightforward, but what they come to represent develops rapidly beyond that—these are spaces that humans created and developed their own thoughts, feelings, and notions in. Even if those only exist inside our brains, they are still valid and we are still affected by them.

1

RICKER BASIN

A Town Lost

Tucked away between the vast Adirondack Mountains of New York and the tall, windy White Mountains of New Hampshire sits the small state of Vermont. While it may be brimming with postcard perfect towns, ski resorts, and world-class breweries, this state is considered one of the most rural in the country.

Take a jaunt into the winding back roads of the green mountain state and you will start to see remnants of the past reveal themselves on dusty roadsides and deep in the trees. Every town has its local legend—prospectors gone bankrupt, murder mysteries, and natural disasters. We even have our own triangle where weird stuff happens.

Before Vermont received statehood in 1791, it was its own independent republic for fourteen years. Since then, that spirit of independence and self-sustainability has lived on and made this state a unique haven for those looking for peace and escape.

Life was never straight-forward. Winter brought paralyzing snowstorms, and spring offered little relief. We call it mud season here. Despite Mother Nature doing her best to deter, the pioneers of the past settled this rocky ground and made it their home. Some of these first settlers had the audacity to carve out their existence in narrow gulfs and gores, and high up on the mountainsides. What they have left behind is now ours to find, explore, and learn from in modern times.

Many of these places end up abandoned in the same way. The owners pass away, move on, or the property goes into limbo one way or another. There they remain for decades, slowly being reclaimed by nature. Some have a different, more tragic history, like the town of Ricker Basin.

Joseph Ricker established the community back in 1816, on the side of a mountain between the towns of Waterbury and Bolton. After a series of devastating floods, murders, and general misfortune, the town was seized by the state under eminent domain in order to build the Waterbury Reservoir, which was completed in 1938. Some structures still exist below the waterline. Years back, the reservoir was drained in order to make repairs on the dam. As the water level dropped, stone foundations and roadways could be seen.

On the surface, a single building—the Almeron Goodell House—still stands high up on the mountainside. Its companions are the dozens of stone foundations, lumber mill sites, and graveyards that dot the landscape.

Built on borrowed time
this house stands out
amongst the cellar holes
of Ricker Basin
clinging to the banks of a brook
accented with broken glass
and a pinch of asbestos dust

Right: There was quite the assortment of equipment at one of the lumbermill sites. Everything from old saws to an entire steam boiler was left to the trees.

Below: A collection of maple sap buckets and the scraps of a furnace placed on top of a stone foundation.

Mary B. Cole, wife of Rufus Place, who died on August 4, 1862, at twenty-five years old.

There are three graveyards in Ricker Basin, one of which is entirely inhabited by the Ricker family, who were the founders of this community and found prosperity in the abundant lumber that these mountains offered. At one time, most of Vermont was clear-cut.

Leaves of grass like tendrils
creep up your legs and
yellow flowers scent the air
with Summer blessings
of pollen and bees

The only structure left standing is the Almeron Goodell house. It sits on a hillside next to a stream. Like all of the other structures that were in this area, this one has a stone foundation and rough-cut timber beams.

But an uneasiness exists
knowing what happened here
a land devastated by floods
and abandoned because of a dam

Words, memories, and objects are all that is left of this community. Over the years, visitors have decided to add their own to the walls. I try not to see it as destruction but rather an addition to the shared experience of the place.

An entire community vanished
leaving behind this lasting
symbol of their
pioneering defiance
against
nature

Ricker Basin extends into an area known as Cotton Brook, which has become more popular with hikers and mountain bikers over the years. Just a few feet off these trails are the bones of barns, houses, and schools.

Around a bend in the road and through the trees
weathered tombstones stand tall in the leaves
graveyards of grey and brown
scattered throughout this mountain town
connect our world and theirs
listen close and hear their voices in the air.

2

ELGIN SPRINGS

This place has a modestly careered past. It was once a hotel, built on promises of purified spring water that could cure your ailments. The water was actually tested and deemed to be of the same quality of the finest mineral springs in the world. Later on, it became a home before finally being abandoned. Sitting adjacent to a main road in the tiny town of Panton, it has a beautiful view of Lake Champlain and the Adirondacks beyond.

The interior must have been spectacular in its earlier years. Remnants of this past are scattered across the entire house. The light fixtures, trim, and wallpaper are ornate. In the basement, there is a large earthen reservoir where spring water was piped into. There was also a collection of old stoves and furnaces. I am sorry to say that someone has gotten sick of its dilapidated presence, and as of September 2019, this once beautiful house is slated to be demolished.

I looked at you from the roadside
all disheveled and worn
you stood guard over the Champlain valley
for sixteen decades

In the background, you can see Lake Champlain in the distance. At this time of year, it is frozen over completely.

you held your earthbound secrets
for even longer
until a young and wide-eyed businessman
came along and discovered the secret of Elgin Springs

This was a well-furnished house, evident by the shards of ornate glass in the front door.

passed on as myth and legend
and left to degrade
but still inviting the curious traveler inside
for a peek at your former beauty
and a taste of the legendary water

A wide-angle lens is a great way to capture the whole substance of a space. Let your eyes wander around and take in every detail.

sold for scrap and left to rot
your future is gone
but your resolve is steadfast

There were plenty of bird nests in here. Something else has been about too, as evidenced by the paw prints in the freshly windblown snow.

Above left: A view of the Adirondacks to the west.

Above right: The front door was swinging open and shut in the wind.

This is a Colt acetylene gas generator. It is in remarkably good condition for being over 100 years old. Before electricity, people in this part of the country would use acetylene gas generators to light their homes.

Above: I like to guess at what could be in the various jars I find, and the smell I could unleash if I opened them. Some things are best left sealed.

as you wait for the next curious traveler
to explore your depths
admire your elegant archways
become lost in the history
and carry on your story
for sixteen more decades

The house was stunning, and it was sad to see it in such a sorry state.

3

THE SHACKETT FARM

A few twists and turns off a main road sits a farm stuck in limbo. The owner passed away some years back, and the house was left pretty much as is on the inside. It supposedly has a beautiful interior. The barn is a different story; it is abandoned but is still used to dry garlic, which was hanging from the ceiling and all over everything else.

Death is a unifying factor in how many of these homes become abandoned, and they are always families that have lived in this state and worked this land for generations. It is a departure from the old ways as we evolve and move forward. Things change, and change is inevitable.

Knotted garlic mirrors its home, rotted and
brown lashed together by
rabbit fur and rusted nails and
red and white lead paint
tractor tires
tired beams
frozen in place by
this icy snow squall
free to intermingle with
cow patties and sad garlic, creating
witchcraft perfume.

Barns were built with strong post and beam construction, which is why so many are left standing. This is not the one we went inside. It was farther back on the property and too far gone to enter.

This is the side of the back porch on the house, which was locked up tight.

Every barn has its own Budweiser bottle amongst
stale hay and elderly neighbors
the last bastion of traditionalists
claiming the property isn't abandoned
but the rabbits and hermit thrushes have other ideas
calling the darkest corners their home.

Looking at the various medications and supplements, it is clear that this is a cow barn.

VERMONT DEPARTMENT OF AGRICULTURE
CENTRAL DAIRY TESTING LABORATORY

Report of Bacteriological Examination of Water
Test for Coliform Group by Membrane Filter Procedure

SAMPLED BY G. Euguir

DATE OF SAMPLING 5/1/79   SAMPLE NO. 7   SAMPLED BY

DATE RECEIVED 5/2/79   DATE ANALYZED 5/2/79

TYPE OF SUPPLY dug well   SOURCE OF SUPPLY milkhouse tap

NAME OF OWNER OF SUPPLY Ray Schackett

ADDRESS OF OWNER RFD, Brandon, VT 05733   ANALYZED BY Stewart

THE ANALYSIS OF THIS WATER INDICATES:

[X] AN APPROVED WATER SUPPLY
[ ] A CONTAMINATED WATER SUPPLY

COLIFORM PER 100 ML 0

BY: Robert H. Mullen

MUST BE POSTED IN MILK ROOM

Below right: There is always a beer bottle.

This is a place that borders our
known realms and wild ethereality.

A beautiful pair of Ebonite skis from the 1940s caught my eye. Since they were on the ceiling, I had to kneel down in the frozen cow poop and rotted garlic to get this shot.

4

CLOVER-DALE FARM

For years, I drove past this place without as much as a second thought. Located right next to a main road, I always figured it would be difficult to get into. Time has truly left this dairy farm behind, and it represents a growing issue facing every dairy farmer in the United States today: abandonment. The dairy industry is and never will be what it once was. We owe it to these folks and to all small family farms to help them improvise and adapt to a changing world, through education, preservation, and community engagement.

This place is very familiar to me and I felt a level of comfort stepping inside, despite the wind that was banging doors and shutters all over the house. It was like a new friend was inviting me in and showing me their house for the first time.

How many times
how many years
have I passed by
waiting and waiting
for the day I'd step inside

It was a cold, windy Christmas Day. After the morning festivities, I went out for a quick visit to this farm.

The front door is unlocked
the back door is gone
the windows are broken
and the curtains are drawn

Above left: A propane tank on the side of the house.

Above rigt: The back pantry was collapsing into the uneven hillside that the back of the house is built into.

There's a hole in the kitchen
an organ upstairs
it doesn't make music
and need some repairs

Shards of glass were strewn across the floor,
emulating from a shattered glass table.

The basement door swings in the breeze
it creaks and groans on its hinges
as flecks of paint chip off
and stirred dust settles

Above left: Enlightening.

Above right: Ready to get cooking.

I am never alone when I explore these places; someone is always there to tell me to watch my step and share some hot cider—thanks Julie.

There's Tabasco on the stove
concert tickets on the book-covered floor
a pearly light bulb hangs in the musty air
odds and ends are every which where

Above: That is a lot of black mold.

Below: It does not work, I tried.

Further we go
the bathroom is pink
there's toilet paper everywhere
oh, why does it stink?

It did smell in here, and the pink porcelain did not make it better.

The barn is very different
with a mind of its own
it moves with the wind
that tells us to go
down to the milk room
and its impeccable well water
glass jars, oil cans, tools
rust, dirt, cobwebs
the stench of old dairy
cast iron memories
farm center ball caps
buckets and pails
tools of all kinds
to fix whatever fails

The barn felt delicate and ghostly. It moved with the wind and everything inside was muted and monotone.

An assortment of tractors and other farm equipment crowded this shed.

Above: It is incredible how this glass jar exists in such a precarious state in a place of disorderly chaos.

Below: From here, it is clear to see that there used to be more barn attached to the barn, and the hillside that is slowly sucking in the house.

This is a place full of
moldy memories
encapsulated in peeling patterned wallpaper
and I don't know how many more
one-hundred-inch-snowfall winters
this tired farm can take

5

RICHFORD STATION

Richford is a curious town with plenty of oddities. Situated just minutes from the Canadian border, this was once an important place for trains going to and from Montreal, Quebec. The Canadian Pacific Railway and the Central Vermont Railway had an interchange here, and there used to be a large paper mill on the other side of town next to the Missisquoi River. The trains still rumble through, but not nearly as frequently as in decades past. I can only imagine the sight and sound of one of the Canadian Pacific Montreal-bound through freights rumbling through town.

Now abandoned, the station sits on the north end of town. Looming in the distance is the massive Blue Seal Feeds mill, which is still in business and served by the railroad. This station also served as a maintenance-of-way section house, and there is still a flatbed MOW cart tucked away in the shed. The accompanying rail speeder is long gone. I felt on edge here, and the brief time I spent here reflects that.

A place for weary travelers
and fresh legs
to climb aboard
and disembark

The feed mill can be seen in the distance which is still active and served by the railroad.

Above right: I did not dare step inside here. The dripping water throughout the structure made me think I would fall through the rotted floor if I did.

The passenger trains gave way to freight
freight gave way to abandonment
the rails are active
but the station just watches
through its tangle of weeds
and boarded up windows

Above: Rails leading into the storage shed.

Left: I was surprised to find a MOW trailer cart still in here. Unfortunately, the accompanying Speeder is long gone.

Water drips from the ceiling in every corner
decades of paint chip away
scattered papers splotch the floor
and still the sign hangs
waiting for the next train

Next stop, Montreal.

6

THE HINESBURG FARM

Sitting at the base of Camel's Hump, one of Vermont's highest mountains, is this old farm. I have only explored the house, since the two barns are across the street and up the hill in the middle of another farmer's field. A bright red truck rusts away in the woods, and a Cadillac has sat in the driveway for so long that it is part of the landscape. It is likely that the last time it moved was by the hands of whoever owned this place.

Like many of the places I visit, I could not find much history of what happened, but I am under the assumption that the owner passed away and there was no one left to deal with their estate. There are rumors of a treasure trove of antique furniture locked inside the part of the house that still stands.

Up in the foothills
off a winding dirt road
with Camel's Hump looming
and cows around mooing
the doors are locked up tight
and a cool breeze creeps
out of the broken windows

Looking like a haunted house in the soft autumn light.

Summer brings a jungle with it, and this old car has become part of the overgrown front garden. It is much easier to explore these places in the spring and fall when there is no ground vegetation.

An old Chevrolet truck is a few feet into the woods.

Half of this house
is completely destroyed
and a pair of classic cars
rot in the driveway
as tourists pass by
unnoticing

Locked and nailed shut.

Moss clings to the roof
mold eats at the siding
ferns and brush poke through
taking root everywhere they can

A fleeting look through the dusty windows.

Woodland creatures of all kinds
they own this place now
the pitter patter of tiny feet
echoes across the broken wood floor

Reclamation in progress.

This place is forgotten
and will soon be overgrown
entropy's fine work
will reduce it all
to a foundation of stone

Christmas in July.

7

BROWNSVILLE

It was very cold that day, and everything was frozen still. The snow was like Styrofoam, with every step deafening. The shutter click of my camera echoed through the bare trees and vacant insides of this small house.

Set on top of a hill and in walking distance of the stunning Moss Glen Falls, this place is a gem. Built with the classic stone foundation and rough-cut timber beams, the structure dates back to over 100 years. Brownsville was a small community built around the forestry industry in Stowe's early industrial days. The area is now conserved as part of the C. C. Putnam state forest.

Bleached brown wood
and gray cedar siding
windows like eyes
watching the bare brown trees
bend in the brisk breeze

A birds nest hangs high in the rafters
and bits of rusted metal
scattered on the slouching floor
amethyst and amber shards of glass
shine bright
in a barren winter landscape

Rough cut timber beams hold up what is left of the floor.

Purple gem of glass.

8

A HOUSE IN WOLCOTT

It was overcast and humid with thunderstorms in the air. I had to wade through a sea of grass to get inside—would you believe me if I told you I did not find a single tick on me afterwards? This one was kind of creepy. The arm of a flannel shirt was hanging from the second floor like it had the ghost of an arm inside it, and I was waiting for musical notes to start coming from the piano. I do not know much about this place. I was here on a local lead I got that it existed. There is a school bus and a tractor in the front yard, so this must have been a farm.

The most these ivories
have been tickled in a
generation is the
drip… drip… drip
of rain
falling through the ceiling
onto the dusty keys

It was thick in here.

Above right: Bullet holes in the glass.

Above: Some farmers used old school busses as a readymade chicken coop.

Left: Crooked insides.

This house is floating
surrounded by a moat
of shattered glass
cracked boulders
cold to the touch
shore up the foundation

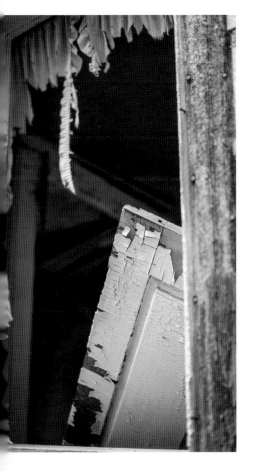

Above: The piano was made by Bailey, a small New York-based company that made pianos in the early part of the twentieth century.

Each step kicks up
clouds of dust
condensed in the
seams of the floor
that is slowly sagging
into the soggy basement

The collapsed kitchen.

9

THE MILTON CREAMERY

I first came here in late October, just a few days from Halloween. The sweet smell of decay was in the air as piles of orange leaves lined the rooms and halls. This creamery dates back to 1919, built by the Whiting Creamery Co-Op. It was served by the Central Vermont Railway, which still runs past in modern times as the New England Central.

Several additions of concrete and brick were added during the 1930s. When the nuclear arms race between the United States and the Soviet Union began in the 1950s, the basement was designated a nuclear fallout shelter. Many rumors also persist about the existence of underground tunnels that run from the basement to elsewhere in the town of Milton. As for myself, I passed on trying to go down there; it would take a lot of fear and desperation to take shelter in those tunnels.

The local creamery is a victim of the decline of the dairy industry. Most of the farming communities in this state revolved around it. Small towns like Whiting, Leicester, Milton, and dozens of others owe their existence to this way of life. They are also towns that just happen to have a lot of abandoned structures.

This place is peaceful and welcoming when you step inside. It was a place of successful business, decline, and death. As the trees and shrubbery around this building slowly wraps their vines and branches around it, I get the feeling that everything here is at peace with itself. The dairy industry has moved on, and so have the always resourceful and inventive Vermonters, to beer and hemp.

Looking out from the second floor towards Railroad Street.

It is never warm in here
the clammy cold of a creamery
once booming with business
has become a canvas
for spray paint murals
and photographer's portraits

Monitored.

The orange glow of autumn leaves
shine through the shattered windows
and blotches of water cover the floors
as ever more drip, drip, drips
through the remnant hanging spindles
of the rusted metal roof

Orange autumn.

Farther up and further in
a preserve of moss and ferns
mold and mushrooms and
a few courageous young saplings
have made a living
on the condemned upper floor

Someone set a bed on fire up here.

Graffiti decorates the walls in every room.

One of the most beautiful rooms is one on the second floor, which is covered in moss, ferns, and saplings. Pieces of the ceiling droop down like stalactites, giving it a cave-like appearance.

Those stairs lead down to the basement which was blocked off. This is where the nuclear fallout shelter was.

A change in season
brings new sights and sounds
snow and ice replaces
rain and leaves
and a chilled breeze
crisp and clean
cleanses the stagnant bowels
of this sour smelling place

It is still in here during the winter. The water that creeps through this concrete building freezes it solid.

Permanence is a funny thing
we see concrete and steel
as having this air of permanence
but even these durable substances
have their limits

The older part of the creamery is in much worse shape than the concrete structure. It will be interesting to watch this scene change over the years.

10

EXIT

Across the fields and forests, you can find them. Remnants of how we made our way forwards are waiting to tell their story. I find most of my locations by driving down a lot of back roads. I always scout a location before stepping foot inside to determine if it is worth the challenge, staying away from locked doors. It also helps to have someone with you in the event that you fall through a staircase or something equally catastrophic happens.

So, take a day to explore your own town. Find that abandoned house and have a look inside. This is where I tell you to be cautious and explore with respect. It is easy to lose your head in wonder, and you do not want to lose your footing at the same time.